TECHNICAL
REPORT

Shaping the
Future Air Force

David A. Shlapak

Prepared for the United States Air Force

Approved for public release; distribution unlimited

RAND PROJECT AIR FORCE

The research described in this report was sponsored by the United States Air Force under Contract F49642-01-C-0003. Further information may be obtained from the Strategic Planning Division, Directorate of Plans, Hq USAF.

Library of Congress Cataloging-in-Publication Data

Shlapak, David A.
    Shaping the future Air Force / David A. Shlapak.
       p. cm. — (TR ; 322)
    Includes bibliographical references.
    ISBN 0-8330-3879-6 (pbk. : alk. paper)
    1. United States. Air Force—Reorganization. 2. United States—Military policy. I. Title. II. Series:
Technical report (Rand Corporation) ; 322.

UG633.S465 2006
358.4'130973—dc22
                                                                                        2006009101

The RAND Corporation is a nonprofit research organization providing objective analysis and effective solutions that address the challenges facing the public and private sectors around the world. RAND's publications do not necessarily reflect the opinions of its research clients and sponsors.

RAND® is a registered trademark.

Published 2006 by the RAND Corporation
1776 Main Street, P.O. Box 2138, Santa Monica, CA 90407-2138
1200 South Hayes Street, Arlington, VA 22202-5050
4570 Fifth Avenue, Suite 600, Pittsburgh, PA 15213
RAND URL: http://www.rand.org/
To order RAND documents or to obtain additional information, contact
Distribution Services: Telephone: (310) 451-7002;
Fax: (310) 451-6915; Email: order@rand.org

Preface

This report summarizes the key findings of a yearlong RAND Project AIR FORCE study, "New Strategic Constructs for Shaping the Air Force." It presents insights developed regarding the likely nature of future challenges to U.S. national security, including both major combat operations against state adversaries and counterterrorism, counterinsurgency, and nation assistance activities. Working from these, it addresses how U.S. national security strategy might respond to the stresses presented by the emerging security environment and identifies critical needs and possible trade-offs for the U.S. Air Force (USAF) as it considers how to modernize and evolve itself.

The draft version of this report, which was published in early 2005, was intended as a white paper input to the USAF's Quadrennial Defense Review (QDR) Analytic Steering Group. While the report's final publication comes after the conclusion of the QDR itself, we believe that our findings remain relevant as the Department of the Defense and the USAF move forward to implement decisions made in the QDR and beyond.

The research reported here was sponsored by the Assistant Deputy Chief of Staff for Long-Range Planning, Headquarters, U.S. Air Force (AF/XPX) and conducted within the Strategy and Doctrine Program of RAND Project AIR FORCE.

Other related studies recently published within RAND Project AIR FORCE include the following:

- Kim Cragin and Sara Daly, *The Dynamic Terrorist Threat: An Assessment of Group Motivations and Capabilities in a Changing World*, Santa Monica, Calif.: RAND Corporation, MR-1782-AF, 2004.
- Keith Crane, Roger Cliff, Evan S. Medeiros, James C. Mulvenon, and William H. Overholt, *Modernizing China's Military: Opportunities and Constraints,* Santa Monica, Calif.: RAND Corporation, MG-260-1-AF, 2005.
- Glenn A. Kent and David A. Ochmanek, *A Framework for Modernization Within the United States Air Force,* Santa Monica, Calif.: RAND Corporation, MR-1706-AF, 2003.
- David A. Ochmanek, *Military Operations Against Terrorist Groups Abroad: Implications for the United States Air Force*, Santa Monica, Calif.: RAND Corporation, MR-1738-AF, 2003.

- Angel M. Rabasa, Cheryl Benard, Peter Chalk, C. Christine Fair, Theodore Karasik, Rollie Lal, Ian Lesser, and David Thaler, *The Muslim World After 9/11*, Santa Monica, Calif.: RAND Corporation, MG-246-AF, 2004.
- David A. Shlapak, John Stillion, Olga Oliker, and Tanya Charlick-Paley, *A Global Access Strategy for the U.S. Air Force*, Santa Monica, Calif.: RAND Corporation, MR-1216-AF, 2002.

RAND Project AIR FORCE

RAND Project AIR FORCE (PAF), a division of the RAND Corporation, is the U.S. Air Force's federally funded research and development center for studies and analyses. PAF provides the Air Force with independent analyses of policy alternatives affecting the development, employment, combat readiness, and support of current and future aerospace forces. Research is conducted in four programs: Aerospace Force Development; Manpower, Personnel, and Training; Resource Management; and Strategy and Doctrine.

Additional information about PAF is available on our Web site at http://www.rand.org/paf.

Contents

Figures

Summary

The Headquarters USAF Quadrennial Defense Review (QDR) Analytic Steering Group adopted the FY 2004 RAND Project AIR FORCE effort, "New Strategy-Based Constructs for Shaping the Air Force," as one of 22 capability assessments. The present report is a condensed summary of that project's findings.

Through a combination of seminar gaming, lessons from historical experience, scenario analysis, quantitative modeling, and the expertise of the project team, this study addressed three main questions:

- What are the key security challenges that the United States will confront in the coming years?
- How might U.S. national and military strategy change to deal with these challenges?
- What kinds of capabilities will the Joint force—and the USAF—need?

Cases examined included major combat operations (MCOs) and counterterrorism, counterinsurgency, and nation-assistance (CTNA) missions.

Major Combat Operations

Regarding MCOs, our first finding is that the "classic" major combat operation—which has typically envisaged combat against an adversary with a second- or third-rate combined arms force that is committing large-scale aggression across a land border—is disappearing. Future "big wars" will, above all, usually be shadowed by the adversary's possession of nuclear weapons (and perhaps by their willingness to use them) and/or relatively sophisticated conventional strike capabilities that can threaten U.S. forces and coalition partners. In particular, all three of the United States' most likely near- to mid-term state opponents—North Korea, China, and Iran—either possess or in the next decade will likely come to possess a range of nuclear and conventional capabilities that will pose substantial challenges to U.S. warfighting constructs. Indeed, our analysis suggests that the United States could fail to achieve its core objectives—could, in other words, lose—under certain circumstances, in a conflict with any of the three.

Success in these stressful future MCOs will require the Joint force to field new ways of rapidly neutralizing an opponent's arsenal of theater-range ballistic and cruise missiles. Some combination of offensive and, especially, effective defensive means will be needed.

Also, the information demands of future MCOs will exceed anything in prior U.S. experience, not just in terms of the volume and accuracy of the requirement but in the time

lines imposed on its collection, interpretation, and distribution by both the likely rapid pace of enemy operations and the vital need to prevent certain specific individual events—the nuclear destruction of Seoul or Tokyo, for example—from taking place. Acquiring and maintaining a comprehensive and up-to-date understanding of any potential adversary's nuclear weapons program and/or deployed force, while perhaps an impossible tasking, may be the ultimate challenge for the intelligence community in the years to come.

Finally, basing and access are likely to become increasingly problematic as host countries fall under credible threat of attack, especially with nuclear weapons. While the United States and the USAF should continue to pursue access and basing agreements with a wide range of potential partners, the USAF in particular should consider whether its force mix needs to be adjusted to enable more rapid, effective, and efficient execution of a wide range of missions from relatively long ranges (see pp. 3–8).

Counterterrorism, Counterinsurgency, and Nation Assistance

U.S. CTNA activities can be thought of as responding to instability and violence through relentless, long-term action to

- *prevent* eruptions of terrorist or insurgent activity by assisting friendly governments
- *intervene* to contain and eliminate imminent threats
- *help rehabilitate* local security, political, and economic conditions to facilitate establishing stable governance.

While most CTNA scenarios will not be primarily military in nature, the Joint force will be called upon to play important, if often supporting, roles in all three classes of response, usually in close cooperation with the armed forces, law enforcement agencies, and intelligence entities of other countries.

For analytic convenience, we can identify four broad categories of resources that will be needed in CTNA contingencies:

- *Finders* are assets—both equipment and, most importantly, people—that provide detailed and sustained situational awareness about a region, its inhabitants, and their circumstances.
- *Influencers* are dedicated to training, advising, and assisting friendly governments and militaries. They also have a critical role in interacting with host nations—both regimes and populations—to help shape their perceptions.
- *Responders* provide important non-combat capabilities and support. Within the USAF, air mobility forces probably make the service's most important and unique contribution in this category.
- *Shooters* bring to bear actual combat power where and when needed.

All four kinds of people and assets—"finders," "influencers," "responders," and "shooters"—will be needed for CTNA. Further, they may in some cases need to be highly differentiated from their counterparts in MCOs—the same sensor that tracks missile launchers on the sparse and little-trafficked road network of North Korea may not be well-suited to

follow a specific sport-utility vehicle into the heavy urban environment around Karachi. Our analysis suggests that across all classes of CTNA scenarios, finders and influencers will generally be the assets most in demand and shooters the least often needed, although it also indicates that a "gunship-like" platform could be very important to provide sustained, precise support to U.S. and friendly ground forces (see pp. 11–13).

Overall Findings

In terms of national strategy, we believe that there is much that will remain the same in the near- to mid-term. The military's role in protecting the nation, while perhaps somewhat more prominent than in the past as a supporting player in domestic emergency preparedness and response, remains what it has been for more than half a century: deterring and defeating threats beyond the borders of the United States. Our analysis also indicates that the requirement to project power in more than one theater should remain a major element of U.S. defense planning (see p. 15).

If the broad definition of the requirement seems likely to remain, what will change? First, the nature of the problem is changing: future MCO adversaries are likely to be much tougher nuts to crack, and their leaders will have more plausible theories of victory—or at least of avoiding defeat—than did Saddam Hussein in either 1990 or 2003. Second, the time lines for our involvement appear to be changing in two directions at once. On the one hand, the United States will need to react quickly to fast-developing events should, for instance, China attempt to resolve the Taiwan question by force of arms in a matter of days instead of weeks or months; on the other hand, success in the "major combat phase" of a future MCO could engender large and long-term assistance and stabilization responsibilities in, for example, a defeated North Korea.

Third, we would argue that a forward overseas presence will remain a critical U.S. policy instrument for both shaping the security environment and providing a basis for responding to problems. However, the demands of CTNA operations are likely to significantly expand the numbers, kinds, and extents—both geographic and temporal—of these presence missions and will determine their size, locations, and duration far more than will more traditional concerns about deterring "big wars." Finally, and almost by extension, our analysis suggests that there may be a need to rebalance the land component of the Joint force to conduct sustained CTNA operations more effectively and efficiently (see pp. 15–16).

In terms of the demands that will be placed specifically on the Air Force, our assessment is that the USAF will in many future contingencies be called upon to undertake such jobs as

- identifying, monitoring, tracking, and engaging specific individuals; small groups; and mobile, concealed, and buried targets
- promptly and rapidly defeating advanced air defenses
- promptly and quickly neutralizing nuclear and other special weapons
- protecting allies and overseas U.S. installations against advanced, mobile surface-to-surface ballistic and cruise missiles
- providing assistance to friendly nations challenged by terrorist groups or insurgencies, including but not limited to training, airlift, and fire support.

Indeed, sometimes all of these tasks will need to be accomplished at the same time (see pp.19–20).

Our work suggests that there are three important new priorities the USAF should embrace as it develops its modernization program (see p. 20):

- First, the USAF should identify how its current and programmed capabilities help establish and maintain a revamped and revitalized "inform and act" infrastructure that will enable virtually everything the U.S. military does, from crafting strategy down to tactical firefights.
- Second, it should consider how it can contribute to solving the problem presented by adversaries' long-range fire systems, especially theater-range cruise and ballistic missiles.
- Finally, given the increasing capabilities of enemy "anti-access" weapons and the lack of available time to forward deploy forces during fast-moving crises and conflicts, the USAF should explore alternatives for rebalancing its force structure to better enable prompt, persistent operations from bases located farther away from the battlefield.

While we were not asked to define specific cost or capability trade-offs, we can offer some insights into kinds of capabilities that the USAF might consider retaining relatively less of versus some of which it might desire more. Five new priorities might be

- new concepts for locating, identifying, and tracking small mobile targets, especially missile launchers and individuals
- theater missile defense
- persistent and responsive fire support for U.S. and third-country ground forces across the full range of combat environments
- long-range surveillance and strike platforms
- well-trained cadres of CTNA finders, influencers, and responders.

Capabilities that the USAF might want to de-emphasize include

- attacking massed armor, either halted or on the move
- killing fixed, soft targets
- fighting protracted air-to-air campaigns
- deterring massive nuclear attacks.

In sum, we suggest that the next Air Force might do well to have fewer fighters and more "gunships" and fewer "shooters" overall—but many more "finders" (see pp. 21–22).

Acknowledgments

This report puts forward the results of a yearlong project conducted by a team of extraordinarily talented people. Although their names may not appear on the cover, Beth Grill, Alex Hou, Roger Molander, Karl Mueller, David Ochmanek, David Thaler, and Peter Wilson are equally the intellectual authors of what is useful here.

RAND colleagues John Gordon and Michael Lostumbo provided insightful reviews of an earlier draft; their efforts greatly improved what you hold in your hands. Editor Judy Lewis was a full partner, bringing order to the somewhat chaotic prose that she was handed. Amy Haas handled administrative needs, both for this report and the project as a whole, with smiling efficiency. To all of these I say, "Thank you."

The credited author can legitimately lay sole claim to those errors and misrepresentations that may remain despite the best efforts of his patient colleagues.

Abbreviations

ASCM	antiship cruise missile
ASG	Analytic Steering Group
COIN	counterinsurgency
CSG	carrier strike group
CTNA	counterterrorism, counterinsurgency, and nation assistance
EMP	electromagnetic pulse
FAO	foreign area officer
FY	fiscal year
ISR	intelligence, surveillance, and reconnaissance
MCO	major combat operations
PLA	People's Liberation Army
QDR	Quadrennial Defense Review
SAM	surface-to-air missile
SFW	sensor-fused weapon
SOF	special operations forces
USAF	U.S. Air Force
USN	U.S. Navy

CHAPTER ONE

Introduction

The Headquarters U.S. Air Force (USAF) Quadrennial Defense Review (QDR) Analytic Steering Group adopted the fiscal year 2004 RAND Project AIR FORCE effort, "New Strategy-Based Constructs for Shaping the Air Force" as one of 22 capability assessments. This report is a condensed summary of that project's findings.

Project Overview

Key Questions

This study addressed three main questions:

- What are the key security challenges that the United States will confront in the coming years?
- How might U.S. national and military strategy change to deal with these challenges?
- What kinds of capabilities will the Joint force—and the USAF—need?

Methodology Overview

This study employed seminar gaming, lessons from historical experience, scenario analysis, and the expertise of the project team.

Key Assumptions

- The United States will continue to be actively involved in global affairs.
- The United States will remain committed to a large number of alliances and security partnerships.
- The "war on terrorism" will continue to be a focal point of U.S. national security for the policy-relevant future.
- North Korea, Iran, and potentially other countries will persist in efforts to field arsenals of nuclear weapons, and some will succeed.
- The deadlock between China and Taiwan over the latter's long-term status will not be peacefully resolved in the foreseeable future.

Structure of This Report

Chapter Two briefly describes our findings regarding future major combat operations (MCOs). Chapter Three covers counterterrorism, counterinsurgency, and nation assistance (CTNA) missions. Chapter Four lays out the implications of our analysis for defense strategy, the Joint force, and the USAF.

Future Challenges: Major Combat Operations[1]

"Not Your Father's" MCO

The "classic" major combat operation—which as typically conceived has involved combat against an adversary with a second- or third-rate combined arms force that is committing large-scale aggression across a land border—is disappearing. Future "big wars" will, above all, usually be shadowed by the adversary's possession of nuclear weapons (and perhaps its willingness to use them) and/or by relatively sophisticated conventional strike capabilities that can threaten U.S. forces and coalition partners. The opponent's war aims may also be more oriented toward punishment or coercion than outright conquest and occupation, which could dramatically reduce the time lines for an effective U.S. response. A nuclear-armed North Korea, for example, will require dramatically less time to lay waste to South Korea, or Tokyo, than it would to invade and invest Seoul using conventional military forces.[2]

Figure 2.1 presents in schematic form our approach to identifying the scenarios on which U.S. defense planners should focus in preparing for future conflicts against states. Basically, the United States must be prepared to fight and win wars in which three components are present:

- Important national interests are at stake
- An adversary state is pursuing objectives inimical to those interests
- That state has the military means to advance its objectives.

---

[1] This chapter owes a special debt to the work of David Ochmanek, Peter Wilson, Roger Molander, Karl Mueller, and Alex Hou.

[2] The point here is not that cross-border invasion can be entirely ruled out, especially in Korea, but rather that there are new, even more challenging cases against which the United States must plan and measure the adequacy of its capabilities. Even short of using nuclear weapons, North Korea's tube and rocket artillery could rain substantial damage on Seoul—and probably ravage South Korea's economic and political life—in a matter of hours. Similarly, China's conventionally armed ballistic missiles are increasingly capable of attacking a range of economic and military targets throughout Taiwan; a devastating attack could almost certainly be mounted far more suddenly and executed much more rapidly than could the cross-Strait invasion that long has been the main concern of Taiwan's defense planners.

The U.S. military has historically confronted the risk of "short-warning attacks" in Western Europe during the Cold War and on the Korean peninsula. However, in these cases, "short warning" typically meant tens of hours to a few days, not the few minutes to few hours that might separate the recognition of, say, North Korea's intentions and the desolation of Seoul or Tokyo. The need to expand these time lines sufficiently to allow U.S. countermoves to deter, prevent, or preempt such catastrophes is an important driver of the need for a new and much more capable "inform and act" architecture, as will be discussed later in this report.

Figure 2.1
Identifying Possible MCO Adversaries

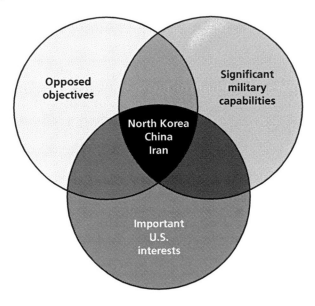

In the near- to mid-term, there are three potential opponents that meet all three criteria:[3]

- North Korea possesses an array of "asymmetrical" military capabilities, especially nuclear weapons, which pose serious threats to key U.S. allies, such as South Korea and Japan. In addition, Pyongyang's record as a vendor of missile and other dangerous technologies represents perhaps the most severe proliferation risk confronting the United States.
- China's growing military capabilities are well documented, as are its differences with the United States regarding the fate of Taiwan.[4] In the mid- to long-term, it seems likely that friction will grow between Washington and Beijing as China's influence in East Asia begins to rub up against, and perhaps erode, the U.S. position there.[5]
- Iran is the most ambiguous of the three candidates. Its military forces are currently the feeblest of the trio, although the acquisition of nuclear weapons would do much to offset Tehran's weakness in most conventional areas. Further, unlike North Korea and China, Iran lacks a specific territorial bone to pick with a U.S. friend or ally. However, the Iranian regime is definitely hostile toward the United States, has a track record of both supporting international terrorism and endeavoring to subvert U.S. allies in the Gulf region, and is striving to develop a military capable of threat-

---

[3] It is possible, though not likely, that within the planning horizon, other states could move toward the center of the Venn diagram—Syria, perhaps, or an Islamist regime in Pakistan. Russia, for example, does not belong, because the interests of Moscow and Washington do not currently seem to clash in areas of vital importance to either side. Shaping events to preclude the emergence of additional possible "big war" scenarios while hedging against the possibility should be an important element of U.S. security strategy.

[4] For an authoritative summary, see Office of the Secretary of Defense, 2005.

[5] This is not to say that conflict between the United States and China is unavoidable but to express the simple geopolitical—or *realpolitikal*—truth that to some extent, power is a zero-sum game.

ening its neighbors (albeit more coercively than via invasion), most of whom are U.S. friends or clients.

A conflict with any of these actors would present U.S. forces with one or more very stressing challenges:

- nuclear weapons
- land-attack ballistic and cruise missiles
- advanced air defenses
- airborne and space-based sensors
- antiship cruise missiles (ASCMs), quiet attack submarines, and advanced naval mines
- unconventional warfare and terrorism
- counter-space and counter-intelligence, -surveillance, and -reconnaissance (ISR) capabilities.

In addition, U.S. forces in all of these scenarios would suffer the full range of difficulties associated with fighting an "away game" deep in the enemy's backyard.

We explored each contingency using a mix of gaming, scenario analysis, and simple quantitative modeling.

North Korea, 2006

For North Korea, we postulated a series of events that lead to a U.S. effort to impose regime change on Pyongyang in 2006.[6] We credited North Korea with possessing 12 to 14 nuclear weapons that its leadership employs in an effort to preserve itself, aiming to shatter the somewhat uneasy coalition the United States has assembled to confront it. When a demonstration nuclear shot over Tokyo fails to deter either the United States or Japan from attacking North Korea, Pyongyang attacks Misawa and Kadena air bases with nuclear weapons, more or less destroying them, and threatens to strike Seoul and Tokyo if Washington refuses to back down.[7]

Our analysis suggests that the United States would have few attractive options in such circumstances. Shortfalls in intelligence and operational capabilities appear to make it highly unlikely that North Korea could be disarmed without undue risk to millions of Korean and Japanese civilians. Further, available missile defense systems (both in 2006 and out to the limits of our study in the next decade) provide small confidence of being able to defend urban areas adequately against a determined attacker. U.S. nuclear capabilities, while offering an overwhelming numerical advantage compared to North Korea's inventory, appear to be of minimal value either in the counterforce or intra-war deterrent role.[8] In the end, the U.S. could find itself caught between an unacceptable status quo (acquiescing in the survival

---

[6] Without going into too many details of the scenario, the crisis builds out of a U.S.-led multilateral effort to suppress the North's apparent proliferation activities.

[7] In our scenario, the initial demonstration attack produced substantial disruption from electromagnetic pulse (EMP) effects but no direct casualties.

[8] There is an asymmetry of stakes at work in this scenario. North Korea is fighting for regime survival, reducing to perhaps zero the incentives for restraint in the means used in the struggle. While the deterrent value of the threat of retaliatory nuclear attack on North Korea cannot be completely discounted, it seems to be a weak thread.

of a regime that has used nuclear weapons) and a profoundly risky alternative (pressing ahead with regime change in North Korea).[9]

China-Taiwan, 2012

We examined a range of scenarios involving a Chinese attack on Taiwan. The most stressing of these for U.S. planners involved the People's Liberation Army (PLA) moving from a large-scale exercise into a short-warning assault on Taiwan. The onslaught begins with large-scale conventional missile and air strikes against military and government targets on Taiwan and against the USAF base at Kadena. Dozens of unsheltered aircraft, including fighters, ISR platforms, and tankers are destroyed on Okinawa; operating surfaces are heavily cratered; critical maintenance and support facilities are damaged; and the base is essentially put out of action. A U.S. Navy carrier strike group (CSG) is in the area, but the multifaceted threat posed by China's modernized military (including modern surface combatants, quiet diesel submarines, strike aircraft—all equipped with advanced ASCMs—and conventionally armed medium-range ballistic missiles with terminally guided warheads) forces its commander to devote much of her resources to self-protection, leaving fewer sorties available to contest air superiority over the Taiwan Strait. USAF fighters based on Guam provide some capability, but the tremendous distance between their base and the Strait limits their effectiveness.

Under the cover of the limited air superiority that it has thus won, the PLA launches "tri-phibious" attacks intended to gain footholds on key Taiwan terrain.[10] Chinese troops seize an airport and a small seaport and seize or sever critical choke points in Taiwan's sparse north-south lines of communication. With the military situation tipped dramatically in their favor, China's leaders call on Taiwan to surrender or suffer the systematic destruction of its now-defenseless economic infrastructure.

Under these circumstances, as in the Korean case, the United States could find itself having only a limited ability to prevent the enemy from achieving its goals. The loss of Kadena and the scarcity of other bases and assets in the region greatly complicate the situation, as does the fast-moving nature of the Chinese offensive (which is in keeping with the PLA's present-day doctrine).[11] The long and short of it is that despite its conventional and nuclear superiority over China, the United States cannot protect Taiwan from destruction.[12]

---

[9] It is worth noting that this scenario is an example of how the Cold War logic of extended deterrence may be stood on its head in future contingencies. During the NATO–Warsaw Pact standoff, the U.S. extended deterrent guarantee to its European allies represented an American assumption of a substantial degree of risk—of escalation to a central nuclear exchange that would have devastated if not obliterated the United States—in order to reduce Western Europe's chances of suffering a conventional attack from the east. To further the Alliance's common interests, in other words, the United States took on a risk against which its partners could not shield it. In the case of the Korean scenario described here, the dynamic is reversed: Japan and South Korea are being asked to roll the dice on a threat against which the United States cannot defend them in service of common counterproliferation goals (suspected North Korean proliferation activities kicked off the crisis in our scenario). The same reversal of the risk calculus may play out in other circumstances as well when, for example, the United States calls on a weak and vulnerable government to increase pressure on or take the offensive against a terrorist or insurgent group that, if motivated, could represent a mortal threat to that regime's survival.

[10] By "tri-phibious" we mean sea-, air-, and heliborne troop delivery.

[11] Some Chinese writings suggest that the PLA is aiming for the ability to bring Taiwan to its knees in tens of hours.

[12] Colleague Michael Lostumbo notes that the United States cannot and should not aspire to "shield [Taiwan] from all harm." This is a fair and important point. However, a successful Chinese coercion campaign against Taiwan would undoubtedly have ramifications more broadly in East Asia, some of which could be positive from the U.S. perspective (e.g., closer relations with actors fearful of a confident and evidently powerful China), but others could be very negative ("bandwagoning" with China by smaller states who reason that a United States impotent to protect Taiwan is a waning power in the region). Whether or not the good would outweigh the bad in the long run, the fact that for the first time since

Iran, 2010

For Iran, we posited not a specific conflict scenario but a plausible set of broad circumstances around 2010. We assess that in that time frame, Iran could pose a serious threat to its neighbors in the Gulf, possessing, as it could

- a small arsenal of nuclear weapons serving as both a deterrent and a threat to urban and other fixed targets within a range of about 1,500 nautical miles
- a number of conventionally armed ballistic missiles, some of which may be quite accurate
- a limited but lethal set of modernized air defenses, including "double-digit" surface-to-air missiles (SAMs)
- a variety of capabilities, from suicide attackers to shore- and sea-based cruise missiles and advanced sea mines, that could threaten commercial shipping and naval forces in the Straits of Hormuz and the Persian Gulf
- control of a number of skilled and well-trained paramilitary and terrorist organizations available for operations not just in the Middle East but beyond the region.

An Iran so situated would put U.S. interests in the greater Middle East in serious jeopardy. While unlikely to be interested in mounting a large-scale invasion of any neighbor, Tehran would be positioned to coerce both the Gulf Arab states and the industrialized world by threatening the world's most important source of energy.[13] The limitations that would make disarming North Korea a risky proposition are multiplied in Iran's case by (1) the vastly greater geographical extent of the country, which would exacerbate both intelligence collection and strike operations, and (2) the difficulties associated with the regime change operations that would have to follow any disarming strike, even if the prior attacks were successful in eliminating Iranian nuclear capabilities.[14] Iran covers almost four times the area of Iraq and is nearly three times as populous; while the U.S. military would likely be able to defeat the (nonnuclear) Iranian armed forces—albeit at some nontrivial cost—the size and duration of the operation needed to pacify the country is almost unimaginable if recent experience in Iraq is any guide.

Key Findings

In all three plausible future MCO cases, our assessment is that it is possible that the United States could lose the war, in terms of being unable either to achieve its own goals (e.g., regime change in North Korea) or to frustrate those of its adversary's (Chinese control of

---

the end of the Cold War a state seen as a U.S. security client had been defeated by an aggressor seems almost certain to have corrosive implications for the American position in Asia and, perhaps, worldwide.

[13] Iran's motivations in mounting such an attempt could stem from a desire to gain greater influence in the Gulf region, to manipulate the global oil market to its financial advantage, or to focus popular discontent with the government on an external enemy.

[14] Absent a follow-on invasion and occupation to change the identity and nature of Iran's rulers, even a successful disarming attack could not prevent Tehran from simply rebuilding its nuclear capabilities, perhaps more rapidly and securely than before. Iran's other retaliatory options, such as subversion of friendly Gulf governments and terrorism aimed at the United States and its allies, would also need to be cut off at the source.

Taiwan).[15] This is true not because the North Korean, Chinese, or Iranian militaries are fair matches for the United States in a stand-up fight—far from it. This is true because future MCOs *will not be* stand-up fights. Both current and programmed U.S. forces appear to face serious difficulties against adversaries who meet one or more of the following criteria:

- Have nuclear weapons and are willing to use them to achieve their goals
- Can credibly threaten U.S. power projection forces and bases
- Can pose threats to key U.S. allies against which the United States can offer minimal protection
- Are fighting on compressed time lines that preclude bringing to bear the full weight of U.S. military superiority.

Thus, our analysis makes clear that developing ways to rapidly neutralize an opponent's arsenal of theater-range ballistic and cruise missiles will be critical to success in future MCOs. Some combination of offensive and, especially, effective *defensive* means will be needed.[16]

Also, the information demands of future MCOs will exceed anything in prior U.S. experience, not just in terms of the volume and accuracy of the requirement but in the time lines imposed on its collection, interpretation, and distribution by both the likely rapid pace of enemy operations and the vital need to prevent certain specific individual events—the nuclear devastation of Seoul or Tokyo, for example—from taking place. Acquiring and maintaining a comprehensive and up-to-date understanding of any potential adversary's nuclear weapons program and/or deployed force, while perhaps an impossible tasking, may be the ultimate challenge for the intelligence community in the years to come.

Finally, basing and access are likely to become increasingly problematic as host countries fall under credible threat of attack, especially with nuclear weapons. However stalwart an ally might be, there is a point at which the potential price of cooperating with the United States will likely outweigh even the most sincere desire to fulfill alliance commitments or remain in Washington's good graces, especially when the U.S. can do little to reduce the risks. This suggests that while the United States and the USAF should continue to pursue access and basing agreements with a wide range of potential partners, the USAF in particular should consider whether its force mix needs to be adjusted to enable more rapid, effective, and efficient execution of a wide range of missions from relatively long ranges.

---

[15] These findings are, of course, scenario specific; we do not mean to say that the United States. *would*, or *must*, fail in these or any other contingencies. The point that we wish to convey is that it is now fairly easy to devise scenarios in which the United States "loses" a war, something that seemed impossible during the post-Cold War era.

[16] This focus on the missile threat should not be read as indicating that the U.S. armed forces will encounter no other difficult challenges in a future MCO. China, for example, fields or is developing a number of capabilities (for sea-denial, air defense, and for countering space-based platforms) that would endanger existing U.S. concepts for power projection in a Taiwan scenario. We emphasize the missile problem because of its extent (all three of our candidate MCOs are against missile-armed opponents), its potential magnitude (especially when the missiles are fitted with nuclear warheads), the enormous gap between the threat posed by enemy missiles and our ability to defend against it, and the profound strategic—not just operational—implications of that lack of capability.

Counterterrorism, Counterinsurgency, and Nation Assistance[1]

The specter of a protracted war with radical Islamic terrorists and insurgents haunts the planning future. While MCO threats can be defined and specified to some degree, the demands of CTNA must of necessity be addressed somewhat more abstractly.[2] Four things seem clear, however, from our examination of the subject. First, regions of instability and limited, failed, or absent governance are potential sources of real threat to the United States. Second, terrorist groups are the epitome of "think local, act global," exploiting conditions and grievances in their neighborhoods to pose threats far more broadly. Third, one critical goal of U.S. policy should therefore be to prevent future 9/11s by preventing future Afghanistans—helping prevent other countries from becoming hosts, whether welcoming or unwilling, for terrorist groups. Fourth, success in these undertakings will require prolonged and intimate cooperation with other countries' political, legal, and military infrastructures.

Prevention, Intervention, and Rehabilitation[3]

When thought of in this way, CTNA may more resemble a public health problem than it does a traditional military operation, let alone an MCO. Like an infectious disease, CTNA problems present widespread and protracted challenges, and the hope for a truly decisive victory over the antagonist—"eradication"—may long remain a distant prospect. In any event, U.S. CTNA actions can be thought of as responding to an "epidemic" of instability and violence through *relentless, long-term action* to

- *prevent* eruptions of terrorist or insurgent activity by assisting friendly governments in the "preclinical" phase
- *intervene* to contain and eliminate imminent threats or "outbreaks" if a problem should become acute
- *help rehabilitate* local security, political, and economic circumstances to facilitate establishing stable governance.

---

[1] The analysis and insights reported in this chapter are largely the work of Beth Grill, David Thaler, and David Ochmanek.

[2] We include counterinsurgency (COIN) within the "nation assistance" component of this construct, which we will refer to as "CTNA."

[3] As colleague John Gordon points out, it is important to note that not all CTNA operations will include any combat elements whatsoever. Humanitarian relief operations in permissive environments are an example.

These are all tasks that will call upon resources from every corner of the public and private sectors of U.S. society; indeed, in many ways, they are not primarily "military" jobs. However, the military *will* be called upon to play important, if often supporting, roles in all three classes of response.

Prevention

Prevention hinges on sustained, low-level engagement and only the episodic application of force, at least on the part of the United States. The U.S. objective will be to shape the environment in "target" countries to deny sanctuary and breeding ground to terror groups or insurgencies. To do so, the United States and its partners will seek to foster competent security forces within the friendly host government(s), assist those forces in eliminating "bad guys," and discourage other states from aiding or abetting the targeted group(s).

These operations will require fairly small but very protracted commitments of U.S. resources at multiple places around the world simultaneously. "Finders"—personnel and hardware dedicated to locating, differentiating, tracking, and targeting the adversary—and "influencers"—trained to inform, advise and assist friendly populations, governments, and security organizations—will be in high demand from start to finish of prevention campaigns. The "responders" who provide critical noncombat capabilities—civil engineers, medical and dental teams, mobility forces, and the like—will be needed to supplement host nation capabilities and to support U.S. actions, but American "shooters," whether "bomb-droppers" or "trigger-pullers," should be called upon only rarely.

Intervention

Intervention scenarios will be driven by the need to eliminate an imminent threat to the interests of the United States or a friendly regime. Such cases could span a wide range of contingencies, from the elimination of a specific individual or target to the takedown of a regime that is playing host to a terrorist group (like the Taliban in pre-9/11 Afghanistan) or securing the nuclear arsenal of a country whose weak central government is at risk of collapse. Intervention scenarios are likely to be relatively short in duration, at least in comparison to either "prevention" or, as we will see, "rehabilitation" operations, but could also be fairly intense and might erupt with little or no notice. Indeed, in some cases, U.S. forces might confront some of the same challenges seen in higher-end MCO scenarios, such as the need to fight through fairly sophisticated defenses to reach terrorist-related targets in the interior of a state like Syria or Iran. Thus, all categories of CTNA capabilities—finders, influencers, responders, and shooters—will be in some demand, although our assessment is that the "finders" will be called upon for the most sustained and stressful taskings.

Rehabilitation

Rehabilitation missions can combine the most challenging aspects of each of the other two CTNA scenario classes. In these operations, the U.S. goal is to put in place and sustain a stable, non-hostile regime that will eventually require minimal assistance to maintain effective governance of its territory.[4] Often, "rehabilitation" operations will be linked to actions in one of the other categories; they could follow either a failure of "prevention" or a successful "intervention." Indeed, planning for the subsequent rehabilitation phase should be a critical

---

[4] Ongoing COIN operations in Iraq fall into this category.

part of preparing for any operation that might result in the need for such a sustained commitment.

As the U.S. has learned through often-bitter experience in Afghanistan and, especially, in Iraq, rehabilitation operations can require large commitments of U.S. and coalition assets, especially ground forces, for a very protracted period of time.

Finders, Influencers, Responders, and Shooters

Each of these three classes of response (prevention, intervention, rehabilitation) to CTNA contingencies will require unique mixes of people and capabilities. For analytic convenience, we can define four broad categories of resources that will be needed.

- *Finders* are assets—both equipment and, most importantly, people—that provide deep and sustained situational awareness about a region, its inhabitants, and their circumstances. Operationally, finders locate, track, differentiate, and target; to be effective, they require prolonged exposure to and familiarity with their target regions and, often, with groups and individuals.
- *Influencers* are dedicated to training, advising, and assisting friendly governments and militaries. They also have a critical role in interacting with host nations—both regimes and populations—to help shape their perceptions.[5]
- *Responders* provide important non-combat capabilities and support. Within the USAF, air mobility forces probably make the service's most important and unique contribution in this category, but other assets—medical and dental teams, civil engineers, and so forth—are also important players.
- *Shooters* bring to bear actual combat power where and when needed.

Finders, influencers, and responders will all be in great demand throughout the duration of the campaign, as will shooters—although the latter might well find themselves acting in one of the other three roles far more often than they engage in combat.[6] While the qualities of precision, responsiveness, and persistence will be useful across the full range of CTNA missions (indeed, across almost all future U.S. military operations), they will be especially necessary in these operations, where extremely strict rules of engagement will need to be followed for a very long time against opponents who will themselves most likely display little regard for the Geneva Conventions. These requirements will render still more stressful what is in and of itself an extremely challenging mission.

---

[5] While our discussion here focuses on a specialized role, it is important to note that every airman at one or more points in his/her career will probably be thrust into the role of a *de facto* "influencer." Whether stationed in or deployed to a foreign country or just socializing with a foreign counterpart after classes at a service school, every interaction with non-American citizens is an opportunity to influence their understanding and opinion of not just the U.S. military but of our nation's values, goals, and behavior. Inculcating this responsibility into every service member will be an important and necessary part of any successful "strategic communications" campaign, especially one aimed at targets whose basic understanding of the United States may be limited or distorted.

[6] Perhaps even more difficult, shooters may need to toggle between their roles as finders, influencers, or responders and their combat functions and back again quite literally at a moment's notice. Preparing troops to perform in this way, and having them do so reliably over a long period of time under terrific stress, has proven to be one of the great challenges of counterinsurgency and represents a new and important challenge for the services' training infrastructures.

Key Findings

All four kinds of people and assets—finders, influencers, responders, and shooters—will be needed across the board for CTNA. Further, they may in some cases need to be highly differentiated from their counterparts in MCOs: The same sensor that tracks missile launchers on the sparse and little-trafficked road network of North Korea may not be well-suited to follow a specific sport-utility vehicle into the heavy urban environment around Karachi. Similarly, an analyst trained to locate and assess underground nuclear facilities in Iran may not be the same individual responsible for tracking and understanding the movements of senior Hezbollah leaders in the same real estate. Even within the CTNA mission arena, prevention, intervention, and rehabilitation scenarios will require their own idiosyncratic mixes of capabilities, and the optimal mix will vary dynamically over time within any one scenario. All of these factors add complexity to the calculus of how much of what capabilities the Joint force—and the Air Force—need.

Figure 3.1 shows a broad-brush assessment of how much demand there seems likely to be for each of the four kinds of capability across the three CTNA scenario classes. Our analysis suggests that finders and influencers will generally be the assets most in demand, and shooters the least.

The USAF will certainly be called upon to provide its share of all four. Persistent imagery and communications intelligence over broad areas will be especially critical, and the USAF will likely need to both expand and "retune" its suite of ISR people and systems to perform in the CTNA arena. This will be as much an issue of exploiting human capital as one of harnessing technology, if not more of one. Influencers will need to be drawn from a wide range of career fields; however, the function is of such importance that each service, including the USAF, may want to consider establishing a real career path for cadres of influencers, to include intensive language and area studies training. At the very least, the USAF's foreign area officer (FAO) corps needs to be expanded, its level of training and preparation

Figure 3.1
Demand for Capabilities in CTNA Scenarios

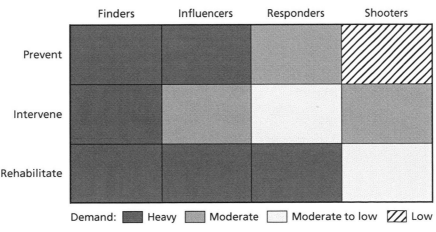

increased, and service as a FAO should not be an interruption in the career and promotion progression in the individual's own career field.

Among responders, our assessment is that the mobility forces will be especially heavily tasked. The other services, particularly the Army, can provide engineering units, medical support, and so on, but only the USAF can bring to bear prompt, scalable delivery capabilities that can avoid insecure land routes and rapidly move people, equipment, and supplies into remote and dangerous areas at (relatively) low risk. Regardless of how the ongoing debate over asset ownership is resolved, acquiring some number of airlifters able to efficiently carry modest payloads into and out of very primitive airstrips is certainly worth considering.

The demand for USAF combat forces will be highly situation and time dependent in future CTNA scenarios. Our analysis suggests that assets capable of supporting covert, small unit operations will be very valuable, as will systems that can provide persistent fire and sensor support. A "gunship-like" platform could be very important in CTNA.[7]

Finally, we would note that future CTNA operations will probably require that USAF personnel be deployed to a wide variety of locations, often in smaller numbers than has been the historic norm, for long periods of time. It is the nature of CTNA that most often these people will be living and working in places where some proportion of the "locals" are opposed to the goals of the United States and are willing to resort to violence to frustrate them. This steady stream of small, protracted deployments into risky situations will create new force protection and mission assurance risks that the Air Force will need to address or be prepared to accept.

---

[7] By *gunship-like*, we mean a weapons system that combines fairly long range, a reasonable degree of survivability against low- to medium-level threats, a deep and flexible magazine of ordnance, long endurance, and adequate communications and sensor capability to fight safely and effectively in conjunction with hotly engaged, friendly ground forces. Our analysis is agnostic about the exact nature and configuration of the platform(s).

CHAPTER FOUR

Implications for the Nation and the USAF

On Strategy: Constants and Change

Our work suggests that *the basic underpinnings of U.S national defense strategy—protecting the U.S. homeland, maintaining global freedom of action, encouraging favorable security conditions, and strengthening U.S. alliances—will remain largely unchanged in the near to mid term.* As stated by the 2002 *National Security Strategy*, defending the United States against direct attack will remain the nation's top priority. However, it should be recognized that the military's role, while perhaps somewhat more prominent than in the past as a supporting player in domestic emergency preparedness and response, remains what it has historically been for more than half a century: deterring and defeating threats to U.S. security beyond the borders of the United States.

Our analysis also indicates that the requirement to project power in more than one theater should remain a major element of U.S. defense planning. While it may be unlikely that the United States will be called upon to fight more than one big war simultaneously, the expanding array of commitments associated with the war on terrorism seems fated to keep the tempo of steady state operations at a fairly strenuous clip for the foreseeable future, at least for certain elements of the force. Furthermore, as a power with truly global interests and commitments, the United States can ill afford to be caught short if multiple crises do happen to erupt in quick succession.

If the broad definition of the requirement seems likely to remain, what will change? First, the nature of the problem continues to change: future MCO adversaries are likely to be much tougher nuts to crack, and their leaders will have more plausible theories of victory— or at least of avoiding defeat—than did Saddam Hussein in either 1990 or 2003. Second, the time lines for U.S. involvement appear to be changing in two directions at once. On the one hand, the United States will need to react quickly to fast-developing events should, for instance, China attempt to resolve the Taiwan question by force of arms in a matter of days instead of weeks or months; on the other, success in the major combat phase of a future MCO could engender large and long-term assistance and stabilization responsibilities in, for example, a defeated North Korea.

Lastly, we would argue that forward overseas presence will remain a critical U.S. policy instrument for both shaping the security environment and providing a basis for responding to problems. However, the demands of CTNA operations are likely to significantly expand the numbers, kinds, and extents—both geographic and temporal—of these presence missions and will determine their size, locations, and duration far more than will more traditional concerns about deterring big wars. Also, the changing locus of critical U.S.

interests, which are no longer limited to the traditional areas of Europe, Northeast Asia, and the Middle East, will further complicate matters.

As far as force sizing constructs go, our analysis suggests that the current 1-4-2-1 model has strengths and weaknesses.[1] On the plus side, it highlights the post-9/11 importance of homeland security, and it also reaffirms the need to have more than "one MCO's worth" of forces. But in some ways it conceals more than it illuminates about the future security environment:

- U.S. defense planners no longer have the luxury of limiting their focus to three or four regions where national interests, classically defined, are at stake. In a world of global terrorism, any region can generate threats to U.S. security. This reality is driving—and will continue to drive—major changes in the tempo, locus, and type of operations undertaken by U.S. forces in the new steady state.
- As also noted above, future MCOs (the 2) are likely to be very different, and far more stressful, than those for which the U.S. armed forces have planned and have executed in the past 15 years.
- Opportunities to win decisively—in the sense of permanently eliminating a particular adversary or at least resolving a specific scenario once and for all—will be increasingly rare and perhaps nonexistent. A successful defense of Taiwan will almost certainly not preclude China from retreating, resentfully licking its wounds, rebuilding its forces, and trying again. Attempting to impose regime change on a nuclear-armed North Korea or Iran may be beyond the capabilities of U.S. and allied forces, or may at least involve costs and risks that exceed U.S. and allied tolerance levels.
- Finally, 1-4-2-1 does not give adequate weight to the kinds of sustained, low-level operations that are critical to the prevention class of CTNA scenarios, which are the ones that offer the greatest potential leverage and may prove to be the most numerous. A new construct should render visible this important class of activities.[2]

Shaping the Future Joint Force

This study has focused on assessing the nature of future challenges to U.S. security, and in doing so we have developed the set of insights about future MCOs and CTNA operations outlined above. We did not seek to perform quantitative trade-off analyses or to develop and evaluate force structure alternatives. Nonetheless, we believe some fairly clear implications have emerged in both areas.

If our description of future MCOs is more or less accurate, two points become clear. First, time lines for response are likely to be much shorter than the United States is used to. Historically, the United States either rolls in on conflicts that are well under way (for example, the two world wars) or begins them in its own time and on its own terms, whether at its

---

[1] The identifier 1-4-2-1 is the force-sizing model advanced by the Bush administration. It posits the requirement for the U.S. military to: protect the homeland (1-), deter forward presence in and from four key regions (Europe, the Middle East and South Asia, Northeast Asia, and the East Asian littoral) (-4), swiftly defeat aggression in two overlapping contingencies (-2-), and win decisively (e.g., impose regime change) in one (-1).

[2] The current author and several colleagues propose such a new construct Hoehn et al. (forthcoming).

own initiative (for example, Iraqi Freedom) or in response to some unacceptable event (for example, Desert Storm and Enduring Freedom). The one case over the past century in which the United States has had to respond quickly to an unanticipated major conflict was Korea in 1950. In that instance, military disaster was narrowly averted—in large part only because we confronted a primitive adversary—and our ally, South Korea—suffered grievous harm in the process. If this experience is more akin to what the future holds than is, say, the 1991 Gulf War—and we believe that it is—the U.S. image of and approach to MCOs probably needs to be revised.[3]

Also, future MCO adversaries will likely possess capabilities, such as nuclear weapons, which can threaten a wide range of targets, including U.S. power projection bases and assets. These present two challenges: first, left uncountered, they could invalidate much of the Joint force's concept for fighting major wars against state opponents. Second, they create a new and very stressful demand to limit damage to U.S. friends and allies. In some scenarios—a North Korean fight for regime survival (instead of the more traditional model of the "second Korean War" being a replay of the first) or in a Chinese or Iranian coercion campaign against Taiwan or the Gulf Arab states, respectively, the adversary may believe that it can quickly achieve its objectives solely through the use, or threatened use, of strikes of various types (including special operations forces [SOF] or terrorist attacks). This implies that the U.S. and its allies will face, first and foremost, the need to rapidly and promptly suppress the effects of these fires, probably through a combination of eliminating them at their sources and providing effective defenses against them.[4] Indeed, in these cases, the promptness of the response—being able to limit the damage inflicted immediately, perhaps even preemptively—may prove to be more important than the speed with which the threat is neutralized once countermeasures commence.[5] Being able to perfectly protect the rubble of Tokyo or the wreckage of Ras Tanura is less important than minimizing the damage in the first place.

A second major point has to do with the role of U.S. ground maneuver forces in future MCOs. To the extent that our enemies' strategies are, understandably, moving away from invasions and toward strikes, *U.S. ground forces also face a changing role*. In the China-Taiwan MCO, U.S. maneuver forces clearly play almost no role, unless one imagines a full-scale U.S. attempt to liberate Taiwan after first failing to successfully defend it. For Korea and Iran, heavy U.S. ground forces appear to come into play either to seize and control limited portions of the enemy's territory or in the context of a regime-change campaign. Ongoing operations in Iraq argue that while U.S. Army and Marine forces were extremely well suited to the combat phase of the campaign, they have proven less than ideal for the protracted "rehabilitation" operation, which (inevitably) follows success in the intervention

---

[3] Of course the United States was long postured to respond rapidly to Soviet aggression in Europe and remains so postured in South Korea. Even in these cases, however, plans called for deploying the majority of the forces that would be needed for the fight during what was usually expected to be a fairly protracted period of strategic warning.

[4] Offensive action against an adversary's strike capabilities can carry with it a risk of escalation. China, for example, has or will soon have an array of capabilities that enable it to strike U.S. allies and even some U.S. territory. U.S. planners should be aware that attacking targets on the Chinese mainland could very likely prompt Beijing to expand the war to targets in areas that the United States would prefer to keep as sanctuaries, like Japan and Guam.

[5] Here we are using the term *preemptive* in its classic sense, as attacking first to defeat an imminent threat. The distinction between "preemptive" and "preventive attacks, and the implications for the U.S. military of an increased reliance on such strategies, is analyzed in Mueller et al. (forthcoming).

phase. The Joint force might well benefit from a rebalancing of land force competencies away from an almost exclusive focus on high-tempo, intensive force-on-force battles against a combined arms foe toward a more balanced repertoire of capabilities for MCOs and CTNA.[6]

This conclusion is reinforced by our analysis of CTNA missions—especially of the prevention and rehabilitation variety—which suggests above all else that the military should get used to being called upon for operations requiring prolonged presence and only intermittent application of responsive and highly selective force. More than the other services, the Army (including Army SOF), and to some extent the Marines, is organized and equipped to carry the bulk of the burden in this realm. This is not to say that the USAF escapes scot-free—far from it. CTNA is in great measure about "boots on the ground," to be sure; but the folks wearing those boots will require substantial support from air and space power: from finders, influencers, responders, and shooters alike. And, while the USAF, like the Army, can probably extract great value for CTNA from its general-purpose forces, maximum leverage will likely come from the employment of specialized assets, both human and technical; these will be in high demand from Joint force commanders responsible for difficult CTNA missions.

A New Division of Labor for the Post–Post Cold War World?

All of these factors—the need for prompt and rapid response to breaking MCOs, the paramount need to defeat enemy fire capabilities early in a campaign, the preeminent role of ground forces in CTNA, and the need for specialized assets in those operations—suggest that a new division of labor among the services may be needed to protect the nation in this post–post Cold War world. A DoD-wide debate is needed on this topic, and we offer the following image as a potential starting point.

First, while the two MCO standard would remain in place in one form or another, the Army might be reconfigured to fight only one; roughly half of its force structure would instead be reconfigured and optimized for CTNA. The MCO half of the force would look much as today's heavy Army does and could well benefit from modernization along the lines that the Army hopes to pursue. The "CTNA" units would likely consist of a mix of SOF, "SOF-like," medium, and light forces, with special training and an enriched array of finder, responder, and influencer capabilities at the expense of shooters.[7] This would obviously involve a major reshaping of the Army from top to bottom and would need to be undertaken over a period of years. It is probably worth noting that while we did not put this notion through any quantitative analyses, we see no *a priori* reason to believe that this reconfiguring

---

[6] The Army leadership has taken encouraging steps in this direction, demobilizing some general support artillery and other units to build up its forces in areas critical to CTNA, such as civil affairs. One question for policymakers should be, how much farther must it go?

[7] By *SOF-like*, we mean troops that are very highly trained and accustomed to operating as small teams under hazardous conditions. They would not, however, need to be as versatile as an "A" team. Rather than being able to, with equal facility, undertake direct action, reconnaissance, and training missions, for example, a SOF-like unit might be optimized for only one or another of those roles.

of the Army would allow it to be reduced in size; indeed, it is possible that it would need to be larger.[8]

Air and naval forces, on the other hand, would continue to focus on power projection against state adversaries (albeit much more formidable ones than any confronted since the fall of the Berlin Wall). The USAF and the U.S. Navy (USN) would be sized to fit the two MCO criterion of the national strategy; these forces are more suited to provide the prompt and rapid responses that will be necessary to win future MCOs than are their land counterparts. Further, to the extent that large-scale U.S. ground forces are called for in these conflicts, their entry into and operation within the theater will be greatly eased if the adversary's most lethal weapons have been neutralized, or at least reduced to a low level of capability, beforehand.

At the same time, the USAF and USN would be expected to provide important supporting capabilities for CTNA. As suggested above, finders, influencers, and responders will likely be more in demand than shooters; one way of thinking about sizing the next Air Force might be that the combat and mobility components should be sized to meet MCO requirements while the finder, influencer, specialized shooter (e.g., gunship), and nonmobility responder capabilities would be sized to meet the fairly stressful demands of the new steady state.

One consistent theme that emerged through all of our games and analyses was the need to radically improve U.S. intelligence capabilities. Indeed, even the most well-designed Joint combat force will have tremendous difficulties succeeding in future MCOs or CTNA unless it is embedded in an "inform and act" complex that is pervasive, persistent, and precise. At all levels and across all agencies, it may be that the U.S. government requires a revolutionary overhaul of its intelligence system to adapt to the demands of a world that is vastly different than any that could have been imagined by the post–World War II architects of existing institutions. As our notion of the battlefield morphs from clearly delineated geographic areas to specific buildings or deeply buried facilities on one hand and the minds of civilian populations in far-flung places and of diverse cultures on the other; as the U.S. military is called upon to grapple with adversaries whose intentions, strengths, and vulnerabilities are radically different than those of our past opponents; and as we strive to increase the effectiveness of and reduce dangers to the troops "at the point," the magnitude of the task becomes clear. Senior U.S. policymakers should explore whether or not an ambitious program for revamping and enhancing the nation's intelligence and information architecture is called for. Developing the intelligence capabilities that will be needed to succeed against the threats of the future will likely be very expensive, but not nearly as expensive as losing the fights that are to come.

Shaping the Future Air Force

Because the general thrust of this report is that there are many challenges ahead for the U.S. military, it is probably worth pointing out that the services are, in fact, very good at doing many things, and they are getting better in some areas all the time. For example, the invasion

---

[8] It would, however, likely require some rethinking of the total force model that has governed the Active/Reserve mix since the Vietnam War. If indeed the United States is going to be "at war" for the indefinite future, an Army that is designed to require mobilization to be "at war" may no longer be a satisfactory solution.

of Iraq in 2003 saw the first combat use of the sensor-fused weapon (SFW), which proved to be very effective against Iraqi vehicles. A process that began in 1942—the search for ways for air power to kill moving armor—had finally reached fruition. Unfortunately, it did so at a point in history where, if our analysis of future military operations is even approximately right, it will be strikingly less useful than had been anticipated.

Instead of decimating columns of tanks moving through the Fulda Gap or across the Kuwaiti desert, American national security now hinges on other tasks, many of which are, simply, truly *hard*. Indeed, mischaracterizing—twice—Saddam's programs for developing nuclear, biological, and chemical weapons, and the thus-far fruitless hunt for Osama bin Laden may be more characteristic of the jobs confronting the U.S. military in the future than was SFW's successful debut.[9] The USAF will in many future contingencies be called upon to undertake such jobs as:

- Identifying, monitoring, tracking, and engaging specific individuals and small groups, as well as mobile, concealed, and buried targets
- Promptly and rapidly defeating advanced air defenses
- Promptly and quickly neutralizing nuclear and other special weapons
- Protecting allies and overseas U.S. installations against advanced, mobile surface-to-surface missiles
- Providing assistance to friendly nations challenged by terrorist groups or insurgencies including but not limited to training, airlift, and fire support.

Indeed, sometimes all of these tasks will need to be accomplished at the same time.

Findings from our work suggest that there are three important new priorities that the USAF should embrace as it develops its modernization program:

- First, the USAF should identify how its current and programmed capabilities help establish and maintain the inform and act intelligence infrastructure that will enable virtually everything the U.S. military does, from crafting strategy down to tactical firefights.
- Second, it should consider how it can contribute to solving the problem presented by adversaries' long-range fire systems, especially theater-range cruise and ballistic missiles. For the latter, the natural role for the USAF would seem to be in boost phase and early midcourse intercept; while the troubled Airborne Laser program is one possibility, we believe that it behooves the Air Force to develop other options for participating in this important fight.
- Finally, given the increasing capabilities of enemy anti-access weapons and the lack of available time to forward deploy forces during fast-moving crises and conflicts, the USAF should explore alternatives for rebalancing its force structure to better enable prompt, persistent operations from bases located farther away from the battlefield.

---

[9] In 1990 and 1991, U.S. intelligence generally underestimated the size and sophistication of Iraq's special weapons programs; in the early 2000s, the CIA, at least, appears to have seriously overestimated them.

Clearly all three of these are more easily described than accomplished. What can be said about them is that none will be inexpensive to achieve, and *none appear to be sufficiently emphasized in the Air Force's current modernization program.*

Approaching the QDR . . . and Beyond[10]

The upcoming QDR is a critical moment for the future of the U.S. defense establishment, and possibly for the nation. The world has changed dramatically in the last few years, and U.S. government institutions and organizations have been hard-pressed to respond. For the USAF, the QDR is an opportunity to make the case for a forward-looking modernization program that supports a new division of labor among the services and moves DoD as a whole ahead in adapting to the new and dangerous realities of the emerging security environment. Our research has identified what we believe will be many of the issues and problems that will be keeping the next Secretary of Defense, and his successors, awake at night. The question the Air Force must be prepared to answer in the QDR is, "What are you bringing to the table to help me sleep better?" The answer, we believe, has two parts.

First, the Air Force needs to articulate clearly and concisely the capabilities it already provides that are essential to the Joint force. Four that merit highlighting are

- An unparalleled ability to neutralize enemy air power. No hostile aircraft has successfully attacked U.S. or allied targets in many years, and there is little reason to believe that this situation is likely to change in the policy-relevant future in situations where the USAF is on the scene.
- An ability, demonstrated first at Khafji in 1991 and confirmed in Iraq in 2003, to dominate to the point of preclusion the maneuver of enemy heavy ground forces above the level of company or battalion. This is one of the main reasons why large-scale, cross-border armored invasions have gone out of fashion.
- Unmatched strategic and tactical mobility that enables flexible Joint operations beyond the imagination of commanders even 20 years ago.[11]
- Sophisticated command, control, communications, intelligence, surveillance, and reconnaissance capabilities that are increasingly tuned to support not just Air Force operations but Joint and combined operations as well.

This is an impressive list, but as this report has argued, there are new challenges to be overcome. And while programmed systems such as the F/A-22 will make sizeable contributions to addressing these challenges, taken either individually or *in toto*, they appear to be only a start. Entirely new or much accelerated initiatives are almost certainly needed. In other

---

[10] The research and writing of this report were completed before the formal beginning of the most recent QDR. While this final version of the report is seeing print only after the QDR's completion (as noted in the Preface, a draft version was made available to USAF decisionmakers much earlier), we are convinced that our findings remain relevant and important. In some cases, our analysis reinforces judgments made and decisions taken by the Department of Defense in the QDR; in other areas, we believe that our work points toward places where the review may not have gone far enough in anticipating the future demands confronting the U.S. military. Both are useful contributions to what will be a continuing debate on how best to "transform" the American military enterprise, a debate in which this QDR marks an important landmark, but nothing like an endpoint.

[11] Between its investments in Joint-use space systems and mobility, the USAF probably spends a larger proportion of its budget on purple (i.e., Joint) enablers than do the rest of the services combined.

words, to sustain its relevance to the nation's most pressing security problems, the USAF—like its sister services—faces the need to explore very deep trade-offs.

Second, while our work was not asked to define specific cost or capability trade-offs, we can offer some insights into kinds of capabilities that the USAF might consider retaining relatively less of versus some of which it might desire more. At the risk of being repetitious, five new priorities might be

- new concepts for locating, identifying, and tracking small mobile targets, especially missile launchers and individuals
- theater missile defense
- persistent and responsive fire support for U.S. and third-country ground forces across the full range of combat environments
- long-range surveillance and strike platforms
- well-trained cadres of CTNA finders, influencers, and responders.

Capabilities that the USAF might want to deemphasize include

- attacking massed armor, either halted or on the move
- killing fixed, soft targets
- fighting protracted air-to-air campaigns
- deterring massive nuclear attacks.

In sum, we suggest that the next Air Force might do well to have fewer fighters and more gunships and fewer "shooters" overall—but many more "finders."[12]

---

[12] We ran more than a half-dozen games and seminars in the course of this study. It was instructive to us that of all the systems and capabilities that participants identified as being particularly useful or needed in greater numbers, short-legged fighter jets and intercontinental ballistic missiles were never mentioned.

Bibliography

Cragin, Kim, and Sara Daly, *The Dynamic Terrorist Threat: An Assessment of Group Motivations and Capabilities in a Changing World*, Santa Monica, Calif.: RAND Corporation, MR-1782-AF, 2004.

Crane, Keith, Roger Cliff, Evan S. Medeiros, James C. Mulvenon, and William H. Overholt, *Modernizing China's Military: Opportunities and Constraints*, Santa Monica, Calif.: RAND Corporation, MG-260-1-AF, 2005.

Gordon, John IV, and Peter A. Wilson, *The Case for Army XXI: "Medium Weight" Aero-Motorized Divisions as a Pathway to the Army of 2020*, Carlisle, Pa.: Strategic Studies Institute, U.S. Army War College, 1998.

Hoehn, Andrew, Adam Grissom, David Ochmanek, David A. Shlapak, and Alan J. Vick, *A New Division of Labor: Reconsidering American Strategy and Forces to Meet New Challenges*, Santa Monica, Calif.: RAND Corporation, MG-499-AF, forthcoming.

Kent, Glenn A., and David A. Ochmanek, *A Framework for Modernization Within the United States Air Force*, Santa Monica, Calif.: RAND Corporation, MR-1706-AF, 2003.

Levin, Norman D., *Do the Ties Still Bind? The U.S.-ROK Security Relationship After 9/11*, Santa Monica, Calif.: RAND Corporation, MG-115-AF/KF, 2004.

Medeiros, Evan S., Roger Cliff, Keith Crane, and James C. Mulvenon, *A New Direction for China's Defense Industry*, Santa Monica, Calif.: RAND Corporation, MG-334-AF, 2005.

Mueller, Karl P., Jasen J. Castillo, Forrest E. Morgan, Negeen Pegahi, and Brian Rosen, *Striking First: Preemptive and Preventive Attack in U.S. National Security Policy*, Santa Monica, Calif.: RAND Corporation, MG-403-AF, forthcoming.

Ochmanek, David A., *Military Operations Against Terrorist Groups Abroad: Implications for the United States Air Force*, Santa Monica, Calif.: RAND Corporation, MR-1738-AF, 2003.

Office of the Secretary of Defense, *Annual Report to Congress: The Military Power of the People's Republic of China*, Washington, D.C., 2005.

Personal communication with RAND Corporation researcher Michael Lostumbo.

Personal communication with RAND Corporation researcher John Gordon IV.

Rabasa, Angel M., Cheryl Benard, Peter Chalk, C. Christine Fair, Theodore Karasik, Rollie Lal, Ian Lesser, and David Thaler, *The Muslim World After 9/11*, Santa Monica, Calif.: RAND Corporation, MG-246-AF, 2004.

Shlapak, David A., John Stillion, Olga Oliker, and Tanya Charlick-Paley, *A Global Access Strategy for the U.S. Air Force*, Santa Monica, Calif.: RAND Corporation, MR-1216-AF, 2002.

Shlapak, David A., David T. Orletsky, and Barry A. Wilson, *Dire Strait? Military Aspects of the China-Taiwan Confrontation and Options for U.S. Policy*, Santa Monica, Calif.: RAND Corporation, MR-1217-SRF, 2000.

U.S. General Accounting Office, *Quadrennial Defense Review: Future Reviews Can Benefit from Better Analysis and Changes in Timing and Scope*, Report to the Chairman and Ranking Minority Member on U.S. Armed Services, U.S. General Accounting Office, Washington, D.C., GAO-03-13, November 2002.